This Book
Belongs
to

..Moira..Pate.

♥ For Lily ♥

First published 1988 by
Macmillan Children's Books
a division of Macmillan Publishers Limited
London and Basingstoke
Associated companies throughout the world
Produced for the Publishers by
Sadie Fields Productions Ltd. London
Printed in Italy.

British Library Cataloguing in Publication Data
Windham, Sophie
Noah's ark.
1. Bible. O.T. Genesis. Noah's Ark – Stories for children
1. Title
222'.1109505

ISBN 0-333-46218-1

NOAH'S ARK

Sophie Windham

MACMILLAN CHILDREN'S BOOKS

"People have not taken care of the world.

We have been chosen to save the animals and

I must build an ark for them which will float on the water."

And Noah chose the strongest trees and sawed the

wood into planks and began to build his ark.

At last it was finished and Noah said to Mrs. Noah,

"Now we must bring together every kind of animal in the world."

There were so many animals to find –

stripey ones and spotty ones and muddy ones.

They chose two of every kind,

a male and a female of each.

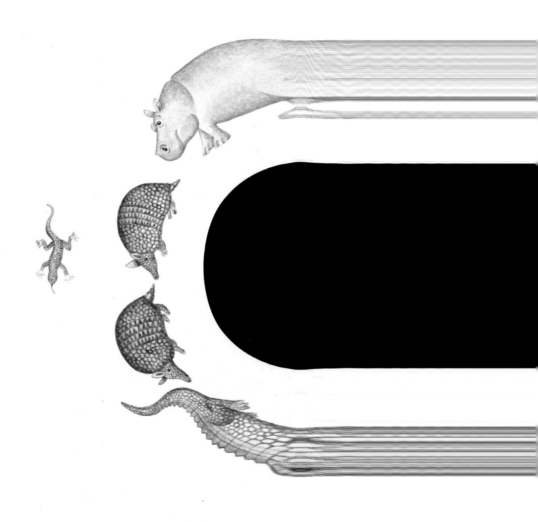

Shiny ones

And two by two they came to Noah's ark,

which was finished just in time.

Mrs. Noah had stocked the ark with everything she could think of,

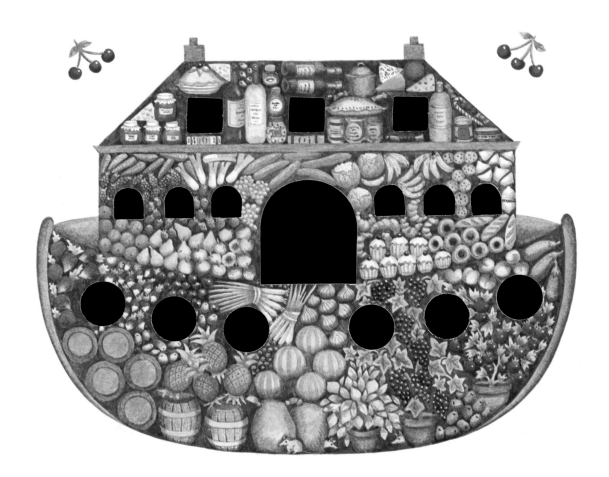

so there was enough for each of the animals.

At last Noah and Mrs. Noah and the animals were safely inside.

No sooner were they settled than

a great black cloud hid the sun.

And the windows of heaven opened

and rain poured down.

And soon,

puddles formed pools.

Pools became lakes.

And lakes became seas.

And when the seas joined together, the ark

floated up on dark and angry waters covering the land.

For forty days and forty nights it rained.

Storms followed gales, and gales followed storms.

Until, at last, the storm became a shower and the shower became a mist,

and then there was only a single raindrop . . .

The next morning, a beautiful light woke Noah and his wife.

It was the sun! The wonderful yellow sun! They dressed and hurried outside.

A rainbow soared across the sky. But for as far as the tallest giraffe could see,

there was nothing but water. So Noah sent a dove to explore

and, in the evening, she returned with a tiny new olive leaf in her beak.